PB&J HOORAY!

Your Sandwich's Amazing Journey from Farm to Table

Janet Nolan

illustrated by
Julia Patton

Albert Whitman & Company
Chicago, Illinois

Tom and Megan hooray!—JN
To my boys, Oscar & Spike—JP

Library of Congress Cataloging-in-Publication Data

Nolan, Janet, author.
PB&J Hooray! : your sandwich's amazing journey from farm to table / by Janet Nolan ;
illustrated by Julia Patton.
pages cm
1. Peanut—Juvenile literature. 2. Peanut butter—Juvenile literature. 3. Bread—Juvenile literature. 4. Jelly—
Juvenile literature. 5. Sandwiches—Juvenile literature. I. Patton, Julia, illustrator. II. Title. III. Title: PB & J Hooray!
IV. Title: PB and J Hooray! V. Title: Peanut butter and jelly hooray!
TX803.P35N65 2014
641.84—dc23
2014001148

Text copyright © 2014 by Janet Nolan
Pictures copyright © 2014 by Albert Whitman & Company
Published in 2014 by Albert Whitman & Company
ISBN 978-0-8075-6397-7 (hardcover)

Printed in China
10 9 8 7 6 5 4 3 2 1 BP 18 17 16 15 14

The design is by Nick Tiemersma.

For more information about Albert Whitman & Company,
visit our web site at www.albertwhitman.com.

Peanut butter,
jelly,
bread.

PB&J HOORAY!

Easy to make,
yummy to eat.

But where does the food come from?

THE GROCERY STORE.

Bread in the bread aisle,
peanut butter stacked on shelves,
jars of jelly lined up in a row.

Put in a shopping cart,
pay on the way out.

Carry into kitchens where sandwiches are made. **PB&J hooray!**

But where does the grocery store get the food?

DELIVERY TRUCKS.

Truck drivers pull up to the loading dock at the grocery store.

Bread in the bread aisle,
peanut butter stacked on shelves,
jars of jelly lined up in a row.

Put in a shopping cart,
pay on the way out.

Carry into kitchens where sandwiches are made. **PB&J hooray!**

But where do the delivery trucks get the food?

BAKERIES AND FACTORIES.

Bread is baked in bakeries.

Flour, yeast, eggs.
Knead, rise, bake.

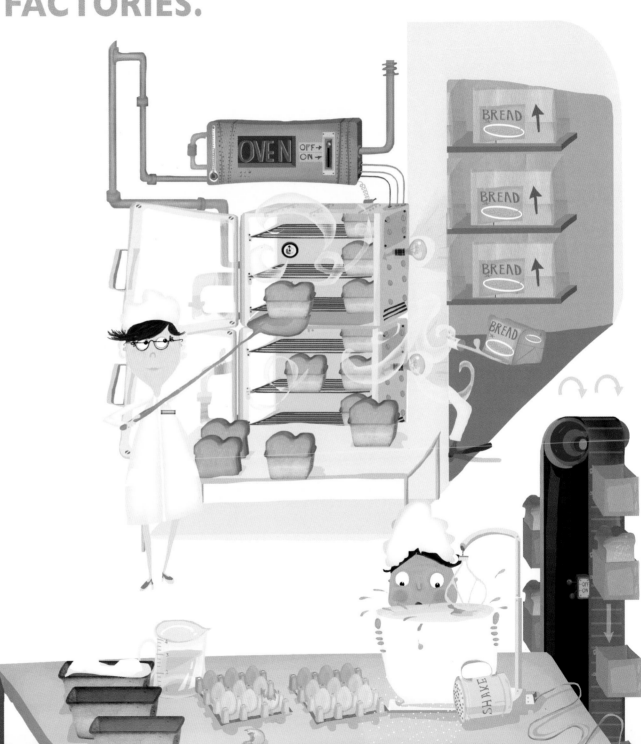

Peanut butter is made in a peanut-butter-making factory.

Shell the peanuts, roast then grind.
Some for crunch,
more for smooth.

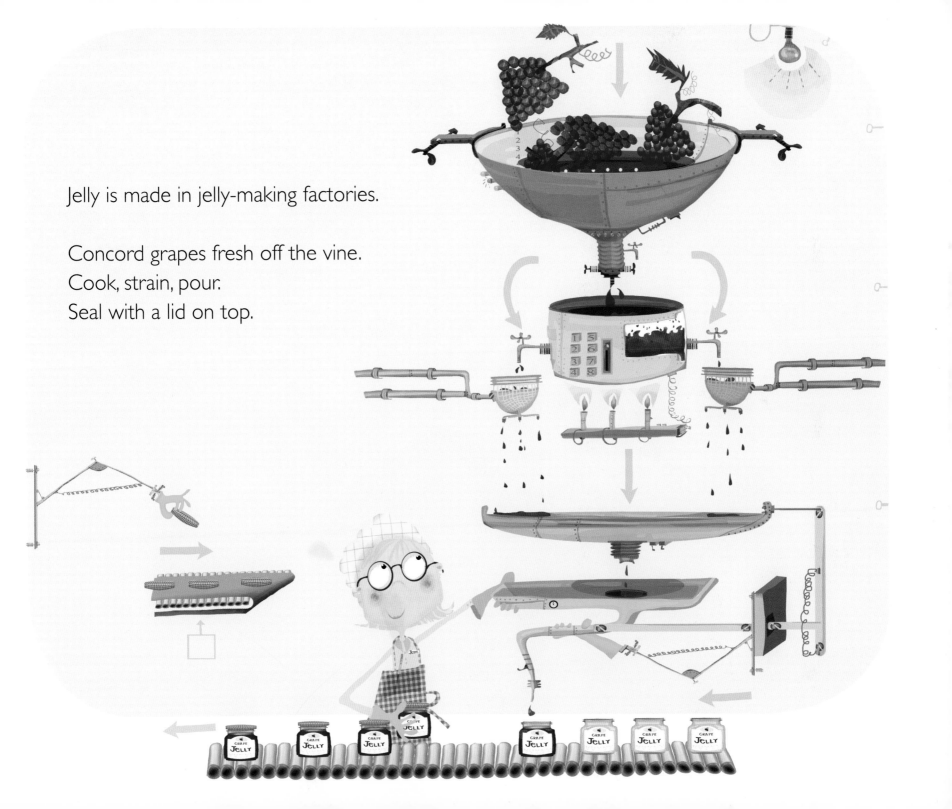

Jelly is made in jelly-making factories.

Concord grapes fresh off the vine.
Cook, strain, pour.
Seal with a lid on top.

Truck drivers pick up at bakeries and factories, then pull up to the loading dock at the grocery store.

Bread in the bread aisle,
peanut butter stacked on shelves,
jars of jelly lined up in a row.

Put in a shopping cart,
pay on the way out.

Carry into kitchens where sandwiches are made. **PB&J hooray!**

But where do the bakeries and factories get the ingredients to make the food?

FARMER'S FIELDS.

Flour comes from stalks of wheat that grow in long straight rows.

Peanuts grow in soil.

Grapes grow on vines.

Sunshine,
rain,
harvest time.

GRAPES GRAPES GRAPES

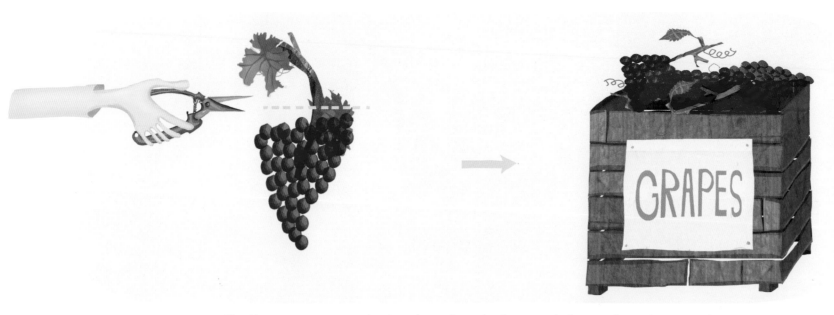

Deliver crops to bakeries that bake and factories that make.

Truck drivers pick up at bakeries and factories, then pull up to the loading dock at the grocery store.

Bread in the bread aisle,
peanut butter stacked on shelves,
jars of jelly lined up in a row.

Put in a shopping cart,
pay on the way out.

Carry into kitchens where sandwiches are made. **PB&J hooray!**

But what do farmers need to get their crops to grow?

SEEDS.

Farmers plant seeds in soil so wheat, peanuts, and bunches of grapes will grow.

So...where do bread, peanut butter, and jelly come from?

Seeds are planted,
crops grow.

Bakeries bake,
factories make.

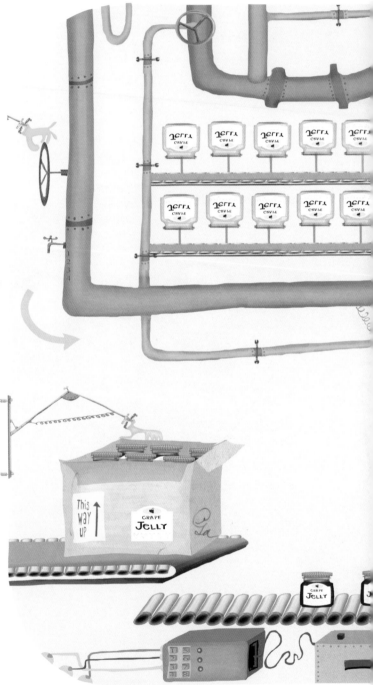

Truck drivers pull up at bakeries and factories, then pull up to the loading dock at the grocery store.

Bread in the bread aisle,
peanut butter stacked on shelves,
jars of jelly lined up in a row.

Put in a shopping cart,
pay on the way out.

Carry into kitchens where sandwiches are made.

Peanut butter, jelly, bread.

It's finally time to say…

PB&J HOORAY!